Social Equity in the Cannabis Industry

Inside Info On How Everybody Can Cash in

Calvin Frye

Preface

As one of the pioneers in the cannabis industry, I wanted to write this book to act as a guide for people who are looking to get into the cannabis industry. Being one of the first African-Americans, to have a cannabis business in the United States, I am more than qualified to tell the real story of the lack of social equity within the cannabis industry.

I will try to offer insights and knowledge on cashing in on this industry with some of the advantages that a social equity license has. In this book, I talk about a little history of the cannabis industry, and how the need for social equity evolved. I have traveled the country, for almost 2 decades, speaking with local jurisdictions, governors, senators, and anyone who would listen on how to write policy, rules, and regulations within the industry. I am the chairman of the Social Equity Standing Committee with the National Hemp Association, and we are doing the same type of education within that industry as well.

Hopefully, you will find this book, very educational and inspiring as you make your journey further into the cannabis industry.

Contents

Chapter 1

Social Equity: My Motivation

S ocial Equity is the new hot-button topic in the Cannabis Industry. But for me, it has always been an issue within the cannabis space. From the first time that I ever knew that there was a such thing as a cannabis collective, where patients teamed up together to grow cannabis to treat their ailments I saw an opportunity for this to become a major industry. I also thought that the cannabis industry would be an industry where people of color would thrive. My rationale for this thinking was that people of color, especially Black people were arrested and sentenced 8 to 10 times more than their white counterparts of which each group used cannabis Equally. So I said hey, this is an industry that I know a lot of minorities participate in to survive in a country that was founded on inequality and slavery. A country that still has systems of discrimination in place whether it's the criminal justice system, the banking system, or the political system. So once I began on this journey, I was excited because I am a scientist, and I always figured there had to be some natural substances out there that could work to the benefit of a person's health. I worked in some of the biggest biotech companies in the industry, and we produced Bio synthetic products that I always thought were unhealthy.

I knew from my scientist days that people were always looking for something more natural to alleviate their ailments. So I've always had it in me as a scientist to look for something more on the natural side to invest my time and energy, and because I believed in homeopathic treatments from a younger age because my parents raised me on natural herbs and eating well from the gardens that we used to produce. I am originally from Cannonsburg, Mississippi, a small town deep in the heart of Mississippi, where we grew our food and killed wild animals to eat, and that was a normal thing and it still to this day in the deep south.

Growing up as a young black man in Mississippi, taught me at a very young age, the discrepancies between the races of people in this country. It was very clear to me at that age, even though I had no idea why things were like they were, but I clearly understand the politics of stuff now. Meaning our schools were literally designated by north and south. The North Natchez school was a school that was predominantly black just like Jefferson High School in Fayette Mississippi where I attended all of my schooling up until graduation from high school. There was a school called South Natchez, where most of the white people from Natchez went to school and it was still based on that same Mason-Dixon line type of mentality. These schools didn't become one school to bear the name of just Natchez High School until maybe 15 years ago, that's pretty sad.

Whether it was all of the management positions or jobs on the white side of town as we called it to the menial operator-type jobs on the black side of town. I always knew that there were equity differences within this world. Once I graduated from high school, instead of taking full-ride scholarships as I was one of the smarter kids at my school, I passed on all the HBCU colleges that offered me a scholarship, and I took a partial scholarship to the University of Iowa, probably the whitest school in America, to prove a point to my parents, my counselors and teachers, and anybody else who doubted that a black person could go to a predominantly white school and succeed. I will say that it was quite traumatic for me during my freshman year coming from a small town in Mississippi where we may have had one white person at my school in the entire 12-year period that I was there, then to go to the University of Iowa where when I sit in the mall, it took a whole hour to pass by before I would see a black person trickle through on their way to class. But to the surprise of many, including myself, I wouldn't give anything for the experience that I gained from attending that university, and going through everything that I went through and seeing all the things that I saw, as well as having many a drunken conversation with my fellow white counterparts. What I learned from the whole experience was that at the end of the day, we are all the same, we think alike. We have the same problems and issues as our counterparts. I learned that it's the system and systems that are in place in the United States whether it's through government, politics, the justice department, City Council, neighborhood council, you name it – it's the systems that are in place that discriminate and keeps other races in the same position year after year.

I say all of that and gave you all that background to say that all of that still applies to the cannabis industry as well. I truly don't believe there's a group of eight white men in some room, deciding that they're going to make sure that there is no equity for minorities within the cannabis industry. I don't think there's some secret mission set into place to make sure licenses aren't given to minorities and women, it is the same systems that are in place that keep minorities in these lower positions and have less equity in whatever venture it may be.

At this point, you may be asking yourself well why the hell did you get into this industry? I got into this industry by chance. Once I moved from Iowa to California to pursue my career in the biotech industry, in which California was a Mecca at that time, I realized that that industry wasn't for me. To be honest, it was the same old systems that I saw within that corporate structure that I saw back in Natchez, as to why minorities and women couldn't advance in those companies. This was made abundantly clear to me after about my second year at the company. This was a multi-billion dollar company that did very well for itself located in Thousand Oaks California. I worked as a research associate in the process development science group of the company as you know with major corporations. You have to keep the shareholders happy to continue to move up in the stock market, so this company needed to finish a product and get it out in time so that when the new year came in, it could use this new product to boost its stock value. I was assigned to work on this project and because of my hard work and getting the samples back returned to them processed, and with the data they needed they were able to get this product out on time. At this company when you did something so good and affected the bottom line in a major way instead of getting your once-a-year stock options you were given something that was called a "Spot Stock Option". Meaning that you were given additional shares by the company itself for your accomplishment. Let me say that I was quite happy and excited to get this award not just financially but as a black man working in Thousand Oaks with its very prejudiced working environment, this was an honor and I felt like I represented every minority at the company by winning this award.

But lo and behold in our ever-ongoing system of racism and discrimination when it came to reviews at the end of the year because I pointed out some discrimination a few times within my department I received the lowest review possible in the entire department that I worked in. At that moment, I realized that systems of discrimination are in place regardless of what you do. So I worked with the federal government and the local NAACP to file a discrimination lawsuit. Thanks to my good friend John R Hatcher III, we led a very successful campaign against this billion-dollar company. Unfortunately for me, that happened in the same year that George W. Bush came into our office and one of the first major executive orders that he signed was to make binding arbitration legal for major corporations. Because of this the federal government was no longer able to prosecute these guys and we had to go through their arbitration process, which was our case being held in front of a bunch of retired white judges from Ventura County, so I guess you guys can guess what the outcome was. But I didn't do it necessarily for myself. I did it to bring exposure to the discriminatory practices at that company. Because that company received a lot of federal money from the Government, the EEOC launched a full investigation into the company and sued their asses off. To keep their funding, they had to do a major rehaul of the entire company. So before I left, they fired most of the people in HR, headed the entire HR program up with an African-American person, and women were finally promoted to major positions within the company, and minority recruitment was up for the company as a whole. So we won in the end... A rare victory for minorities in this country.

This was a turning point in my life as a black man in America. I knew how hard it was, especially where I came from. To be a black man and do everything you think you're supposed to do in this country to be a successful person and a great citizen was obviously bullshit. I worked my butt off in high school, had one of the highest ACT scores at my school during that time, graduated at the top of my class, got an academic scholarship to a Big 10 university, graduated – even went to graduate school. I found a very good job at one of the top biotech companies in the world, won one of the most prestigious awards there, and at the end of the day, will still given the lowest review in my department and discriminated against. So at that point, I decided the next career that I took, I was going to make sure that we received our just due for our hard work.

PRO TIP: Use your anger as motivation – it can sustain you!

Chapter 2

How it all started: from a black pioneers view

After my stent in the corporate biotech industry, a few business ventures here and there, and doing a little real estate, I figured it was time for me to do something that I was more passionate about so low and behold one day my neighbor approached me and told me that he was diagnosed with cancer. I felt really bad for him obviously because he was my neighbor and I considered him a friend as well. A few weeks later he came by and told me that he was doing treatment with chemo and radiation and that the doctors had told him that Cannabis was something that their other patients were using to relieve them of the nausea associated with chemotherapy. Then about a week later, he came back happily with a brown paper bag with some type of receipt stapled to it and told me that he purchased some cannabis from an actual store. As you can believe back in 2005, there was no such thing as a dispensary that was handing out marijuana to people so of course I didn't believe him. I even told him hey man you don't have to be embarrassed and pretend that you purchased some marijuana from some legal venue, I'm not here to judge you if you ended up getting it from some guy in the alley. He then went on and on that no he did not get it from a guy in the alley and that there was this store in West Hollywood, California that was a medical marijuana collective – I believe that was the terminology that was used back then and that this was all legal. I was like OK whatever man and I kind of went on about my day, but I was happy to see that he was doing better. About two months later he came over and he was super excited to tell me that his cancer was in remission and that the cannabis worked not only with the nausea, but he believed it worked with sending the cancer into remission as well based on things that he had heard. I was super excited for him, and I was happy to see that a natural herb was what helped heal him as opposed to synthetics or shall I say poisons like chemotherapy and radiation.

This is where everything changed for me and sent me down the path of a pioneer in the cannabis industry. My neighbor approached me maybe a month later and offered me this proposition to open a cannabis store with him. I told him he must be out of his mind, and that he didn't have to lie to me about where he got his cannabis from. He swore up and down that this was true, and even gave me a card to go and attend this meeting held by Bruce Margolin who was the president of Americans for Safe Access, the local LA chapter I believe back in around 2004. I attended to event, and to my surprise, he was not lying. This was a real thing and there were a few stores in West Hollywood that sold cannabis. I still didn't believe him so about a month later, he opened the store in Tarzana California which if you're from Southern California, you know that's the rich people's side of town.

I told him he must be out of his mind and that that's where Michael Jackson and his family live so they will be arresting his ass right away because they don't play that on that side of town. So he opened up anyway and eventually convinced me to come by and check out his location. I thought that was the craziest idea ever but the mischievous little boy inside of me couldn't resist the opportunity to see if this was real. So one day I went to this location to check it out. Of course, as I walked towards the location, it was in this tall men-in-black type of building where they could see out but you couldn't see in. As I approached the door and it opened, I could smell a little tinge of that familiar smell of cannabis and I was greeted by a 7-foot 300-pound black security guard who looked like he was ready to rip me a new one if I tried anything. Luckily, my partner OK'd me and I came in to check it out. Lo and behold, as the clinic opened and patients started to show up, I, with my many stereotypes, thought that I was going to be seeing a bunch of rappers, skateboarders, and regular old people knocking the door down. But in reality, there were a bunch of middle and upper-class suits and ties, dresses, and heel-wearing white German, Jewish, Asian, and other people coming in and purchasing this cannabis. I was blown away, and when I saw how much money he made in just one day, I couldn't believe it- let's just say over the next month or so after checking this out with my wife and an attorney, I got into the industry. I opened my shop in the next city over, Studio City California, and I called my shop, Compassionate Caregivers of Studio City Cloneville. We opened the shop together but unfortunately, because of some internal family issues on my partner's side he pulled out and I was left to carry on this very new dangerous project, two weeks after I opened it, by myself. I almost closed the doors and just called it quits but I saw so much potential when I saw the types of people that were coming in and using this as medicine.

After I decided to move forward with this venture, I joined Americans for Safe Access, which was a national group that pushed for legal access and safe access to cannabis medicine. This group was headed by Don Duncan, one of the clinic owners located in West Hollywood that I spoke of earlier. This group was responsible for the spark that was needed to get the entire cannabis industry going and is responsible for where it is today. I always like to give the pioneers props because the real people who created these industries, never get their flowers and are often overshadowed by the big companies and corporations that come after them and make billions of dollars.

Anyway, one of the biggest things that I can attribute to putting cannabis on the national stage and getting people's interest peaked was the media coverage that Los Angeles got during a hit movie/documentary called Super High Me, of which I costarred in and a shock jock news investigator from CBS that did a story on a medical marijuana doctor that was giving out marijuana doctors recommendation. The documentary, Super High Me, aired on HBO, Cinemax, and Netflix. Netflix actually paid for the documentary and initially wanted to do a reality show on it but because this was such a hot topic, they steered away from it back then. This all happened when a comedian by the name of Doug Benson, who was known as the marijuana comic gave a show one night and joked about what would happen if he smoked weed for 30 days in a row and did not smoke weed for 30 days in a row, like the McDonald's movie called "Super Size Me", by Morgan Spurlock. A Netflix representative happened to be in the audience that night and approached the comedian afterward and asked him if he would do it if they paid him too and of course, he said yes, and the rest is history.

The other thing that happened to push this industry forward, was when the shock jock did his Rambo-style interview with the doctor in West Hollywood, he exposed the fact that these doctors were giving out doctors recommendations to patients with minor symptoms. Let's just say were not very believable. The funny thing happened was that when I first opened my clinic, the doctor's recommendations of what a patient had to have to come into the clinic that I used to get from people were very raggedy and looked like a high school kid's condom that he had in his pocket for two years. But after that CBS, shock jock's investigation was aired all over the country and all over Los Angeles. Instead of the doctor getting into trouble and people being appalled, this just merely told the rest of the country, and especially LA that there was such a place where you could go and get a marijuana license recommendation to go to a collective to get cannabis. The next day there was a line out my door and people came in with brand new doctor recs from guess who. Literally, from that moment on the industry has never been the same, and once people found out about the ability to have access to cannabis, in a safe and reputable environment, **the industry was born**.

PRO TIP: Don't be afraid of current laws- that's how change is made, challenge the local jurisdiction!

At that time there were only about five or six of us in Los Angeles. The documentary Super High Me chronicles, the actual time that the medical marijuana movement started in

California and spread throughout the rest of the United States. One day a producer of that film happened to come to my Dispensary because he needed a place for the Comedian to get his cannabis and asked me if I would costar in the movie, and that he would also chronicle the medical marijuana movement in Los Angeles along with his comedians 30-day benge. Being the smart guy that I am, I said, of course, because I saw it as a way for me to portray myself as an activist and a scientist, who believed in medical marijuana, and to show it in a good light. I also did this, because as a black man, I wanted to make sure that it was documented that I was doing the right thing so that I wouldn't be stereotyped and arrested later by LAPD. That was the best decision I ever made because I was visited by the LAPD, VICE drug enforcement squads, and even the CIA, most of them were undercover.

During this time, I saw that there was a need to have positive black representation in this burgeoning industry, because of the stereotypes and the criminal justice system, and how we were seen and prosecuted when it came to this particular drug. That was further enforced by, one of my colleagues at American for a Safe Access who told the few minorities that were in this group that if they were approached by the news or someone to call them so they could speak for them because they were afraid we weren't articulate enough to handle that situation. Of course that pissed me off so the first chance that a news organization came to my door I made sure that I did not call them and handled it on my own. Probably three weeks into the shooting of the documentary NBC's main crew showed up at my doorstep, with kind of a lower-level shock interview, but I flipped it on them and the interview happened to go prime time and was one of the most positive interviews that they had done on the subject. This was mainly because my dispensaries or shall I say Collective at that time was like a doctor's office- no smoking was allowed and no cannabis use was allowed. 94.7 the wave, which is a jazz station here in Los Angeles played in the background and my facility looked like a doctor's office with aids and cancer patients working the facility. This made for good news coverage and it went national once they interviewed us.

Chapter 3

The need for social equity: The early years

As I stated earlier, I figured that this was going to be an industry in which minorities could flourish because of our association with drugs via the justice system. I figured this would be an industry that no one else would want to touch, and we would have an advantage in our association with the plant. **Boy was I wrong**. About a year into this industry, the word has gotten around and states like Colorado and Washington were also getting into the mix. As chronicled in the movie Super High Me, the number of dispensaries went from that initial four or five to hundreds in a year! Because of this explosion of dispensaries, it was hard and harder to have good players in the game - drug dealers came out of the woodwork to get into this industry. We pleaded to the city of Los Angeles at that time to put in some type of rules and regulations so that the industry wouldn't Implode on itself and the federal government could come and shut everything down. Eventually, after another year passed and the number of dispensaries in LA hovered around 2000, the city had no choice but to step in and try to regulate the situation. Around November 2007 the city finally requested all dispensaries that wanted to stay in business and operate correctly to come down to the city clerk's office and register their business and bring all the necessary paperwork to do so. Only about 187 out of the several thousand came in to do so and that number later became what was known to be a Pre-ICO. Anyone from LA or anyone who has followed the cannabis industry closely knows that that was the coveted group of licenses that later went for millions of dollars in Los Angeles because they were the ones that came in and followed the rules, and they were the only licenses that the city of Los Angeles respected and recognized.

At that time, there was a pretty good mix of people who owned the licenses. There was a good mix of black, White, Armenian, Jews and women, and everybody else in between.

But by the time law enforcement got involved and started to shut down a lot of the illegal shops, and rules and regulations started to be put in place, most minorities began to fall by the wayside because of the new rules and regulations that came in requiring these businesses to be able to outfit the buildings and do certain things that cost money that a lot of these people couldn't afford. This also was a time when many vulture management groups were showing up on the scene and taking advantage of the Pre-ICOs, who, unfortunately, weren't savvy business individuals to start with.

For about seven or eight years after the pre-ICO permit permitted businesses were trying to get established, rogue, or Legacy as they called them were being shut down for not trying to participate correctly. The state of California finally started to get involved. The city of Los Angeles finally created a cannabis division, headed by Cat Packer, a bright young activist from the Marijuana Policy Project to head the department. This was the first time I saw the language of social equity appear on the meeting agenda. One of the reasons that we started to see social equity start to be an issue in the city of Los Angeles was because the management groups were taking advantage of minorities and women, because like I said earlier, they didn't have the necessary business skills or capital to run these businesses as the city was putting in more requirements, and the state was drafting its rules and regulations.

PRO TIP: Be wary of management groups – your Due Diligence!

Cat Paker Executive Director of the Dept. Cannabis Regulation in LA

As the movement took off in Los Angeles, several other states like Colorado, Washington, and Oregon came online. What I was hoping for earlier, and what I thought was going to be a windfall for minorities suddenly turned into a nightmare as soon as medical cannabis was seen as a legitimate business. After all the hard work from activists, like myself and other minorities to get this industry up and going was overshadowed by corporations and venture capitalists. Once actual licenses started to be handed out because the industry was well on its way to being a billion industry, rules and regulations started to come into play and as I mentioned earlier, the systems of discrimination that are already in place also came along with those rules and regulations. By the time the smoke and dust had settled, well over 90% of all licenses given out were given out to white males. Though I was super disappointed, I wasn't surprised because I had seen it all before, from Mississippi to Iowa to California.

Chapter 4

Social Equity: A Broader View

O nce it was clear, that social equity was needed within the cannabis industry, pioneers, like myself made it clear, statewide, and nationally that we were not going to just stand by and be overlooked for licenses. These are some of the things we push for and the rationale behind it. so for the common person who has no experience in the industry, or doesn't know the history of the calls for social equity within the cannabis industry, historically has come about let's just keep it simple and explain what social equity is.

Social equity in the cannabis industry refers to efforts to ensure justice and fairness within the sector's social policies. It aims to address the historical and ongoing impacts of cannabis criminalization, particularly on communities of color and individuals with prior marijuana offenses. Social equity programs are designed to provide opportunities for these groups to participate meaningfully in the legal cannabis industry.

These programs often include measures such as:

- Prioritizing licensing for minority-owned businesses and individuals affected by cannabis prohibition.

  ○ Providing financial assistance, resources, and technical support to help these individuals enter the industry.

  ○ Expunging or sealing records of cannabis-related offenses to mitigate long-term impacts on individuals' lives.

  ○ Reinvesting cannabis tax revenue into communities that have been disproportionately harmed by the War on Drugs.

The goal is to create a diverse, equitable, and inclusive cannabis industry that rectifies the social and economic harms of prohibition and ensures that the benefits of cannabis legalization are shared equitably. [1]

The role of cannabis in social justice is multifaceted and has been increasingly recognized in recent years. The legalization and regulation of cannabis have been seen as opportunities to address social inequities, particularly those related to racial disparities in drug enforcement.

Historically, cannabis prohibition has disproportionately affected disadvantaged minority populations, with people of color being significantly more likely to be arrested for cannabis-related offenses[4][8]. This has led to calls for cannabis reform to include social justice measures, such as the expungement of previous arrests and convictions for cannabis-related crimes, and the implementation of social equity programs.

Social equity programs aim to ensure that those most affected by cannabis prohibition, including people of color and those with prior marijuana offenses, are given opportunities to participate in the burgeoning cannabis industry[3]. These programs can include measures such as prioritizing licensing for minority-owned businesses, providing financial assistance or resources for those entering the industry, and reinvesting cannabis tax revenue into communities most affected by prohibition.

States like Illinois, New York, New Jersey, and others have recognized the importance of going beyond expungement and have implemented comprehensive social equity programs. These programs aim to address the economic, educational, and wealth-building opportunities missed due to cannabis convictions[1]. For instance, New York's Marijuana Regulation and Taxation Act focuses on racial and social justice, aiming to create equity-building and community reinvestment opportunities.

However, the implementation of social equity in cannabis legislation has its challenges. Some critics argue that the commercialization of cannabis exacerbates many of the issues it aims to address, such as incarceration and reformation[4]. Others point out that the transition from illicit to legal cannabis has not always resulted in social justice, with concerns about the diversity of the cannabis industry and the potential for cannabis legalization to negatively impact the populations that most suffered under prohibition.

The role of cannabis in social justice is a complex and evolving issue. While cannabis reform presents opportunities to address historical social inequities, it also presents challenges that require careful consideration and ongoing evaluation. The ultimate goal is to create a diverse, equitable, and inclusive cannabis industry that rectifies the social and economic harms of prohibition. [2]

PRO TIP: Look to do business in capped markets — your chances increase 50-fold due to lack of competition!

Chapter 5

Participating in Social Equity Programs and Implementation

Participating in social equity programs in the cannabis industry involves understanding the eligibility criteria, application process, and benefits offered by these programs. Here's a detailed guide on how to participate:

Eligibility Criteria

Eligibility for social equity programs often depends on factors such as residency, income, and previous cannabis convictions.

For instance, in Illinois, a social equity applicant must have at least 51% ownership and control by one or more individuals who have lived in a Disproportionately Impacted Area for 5 of the past 10 years, have been arrested for or convicted of cannabis-related offenses eligible for expungement, or have more than

10 full-time employees, half of whom meet the aforementioned criteria.

Application Process

The application process varies by state and program. For example, the Massachusetts Social Equity Program offers a free, statewide technical assistance and training program that creates sustainable pathways into the cannabis industry. Interested individuals can apply online when the application window opens[2]. Similarly, the Illinois Cannabis Social Equity Program provides low-interest forgivable loans, legal assistance, technical assistance, and individualized support to social equity licensees[9].

Benefits

Social equity programs offer a range of benefits to participants. These can include access to capital and financing, technical support, priority application processing, and reduced or waived fees[6]. In Illinois, qualified social equity applicants are given a 50% discount on all application fees, licensing fees, and other financial requirements[7]. Some programs, like the Flowhub Social Equity Program, offer additional benefits such as discounted software for cannabis businesses.

Participating in social equity programs in the cannabis industry requires understanding the specific eligibility criteria and application process of the program in question, as well as leveraging

the benefits offered by these programs to build a successful cannabis business. It's also important to learn from the success stories of other social equity participants and seek out resources and support to navigate the challenges of the cannabis industry.

PRO TIP: Make sure you read the social equity regulations because they differ from state to state

To ensure that social equity programs are effectively implemented in the cannabis industry, addressing the main challenges of access to capital and financing, licensing and regulatory barriers, and program evaluation and accountability is essential. Here are some strategies to tackle these challenges:

Access to Capital and Financing

- **Partnerships with Private Investors**: Encourage partnerships with private investors, including venture capital funds
and angel investors, who are interested in supporting social equity initiatives.

- **Government Grants and Loans**: Advocate for government grants and loans specifically designed to support social equity applicants in the cannabis industry.

- **Community Development Financial Institutions (CD-FIs)**: Work with CDFIs that provide financial services to underserved communities and can offer loans and financial assistance to social equity applicants.

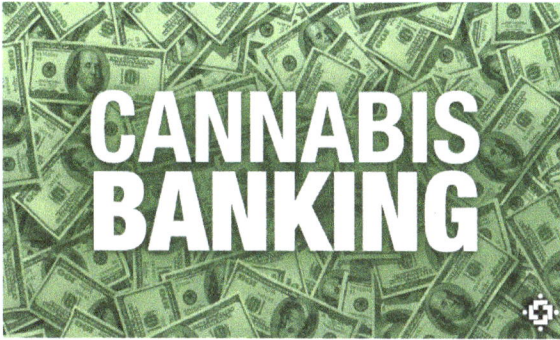

Licensing and Regulatory Barriers

- **Streamlined Application Processes**: Simplify the licensing application process for social equity applicants, potentially by reducing paperwork and providing clear guidelines.

- **Technical Assistance**: Offer technical assistance programs to help social equity applicants navigate the complex regulatory environment and successfully apply for licenses.

- **Policy Advocacy**: Engage in policy advocacy to influence the creation of more inclusive and equitable licensing regulations that lower barriers to entry.

Program Evaluation and Accountability

- **Transparent Metrics**: Establish clear and transparent metrics to measure the success of social equity programs and ensure that they are meeting their intended goals.

- **Regular Reporting**: Implement regular reporting requirements for social equity programs to track progress and identify areas for improvement.

- **Community Involvement**: Involve community stakeholders in the evaluation process to ensure that social equity programs are accountable to the communities they are designed

to serve[1].

By focusing on these strategies, the cannabis industry can work towards more effective implementation of social equity programs, ensuring that they provide meaningful opportunities for communities of color and those disproportionately affected by cannabis prohibition. It's also important to continuously review and adapt these strategies as the industry evolves and new insights are gained from the implementation of social equity programs in various jurisdictions.

As you wonder, what can I do as a social equity potential applicant, to give myself the best chance of being awarded a license? To increase your chances of getting a social equity cannabis license, you can take several steps:

1. **Understand the Requirements**: Applicants should thoroughly understand the specific requirements for social equity applicants in their state. This may include residency requirements, proof of impact from cannabis prohibition, and other specific criteria.

2. **Prepare a Strong Application**: A well-prepared application can significantly increase the chances of success. This includes a solid business plan, a well-thought-out capital and entity plan, and a bulletproof financial model.

3. **Assemble a Qualified Team**: Having a team with the right expertise can be crucial. This includes legal experts who understand cannabis laws and regulations, as well as financial experts who can help with financial

planning and raising capital.

4. **Secure Necessary Resources**: Applicants should secure the necessary resources to start and operate their business. This includes securing approved real estate and having sufficient capital to cover startup and operational costs.

5. **Take Advantage of Available Support**: Many states offer support to social equity applicants, such as technical assistance, training, and funding. Applicants should take full advantage of these resources.

6. **Double-Check the Application**: Before applying, applicants should double-check to ensure that it is complete and that all required documents are included. Any errors or omissions can lead to delays or rejection of the application.

7. **Start Early**: The application process can take longer than anticipated, so applicants should start early to give themselves enough time to prepare a thorough and complete application.

Remember, each state has its own specific requirements and processes for social equity cannabis licenses, so applicants should familiarize themselves with the rules and regulations in their specific state.

Chapter 6

Challenges and Criticisms of the Social Equity Programs

S ocial equity applicants in the cannabis industry face a range of common challenges that can hinder their success and ability to compete with more established businesses. Here are some of the most prevalent issues:

1. **Limited Access to Capital**: One of the most significant barriers for social equity applicants is the difficulty in securing financing. Traditional banking services are often unavailable to cannabis businesses

due to federal restrictions, making it hard for these applicants to obtain loans and other financial services.

2. **Complicated Application Processes**: The process of applying for a cannabis license can be complex and daunting,

with a multitude of forms, fees, and legal requirements. This can be particularly challenging for those without prior experience in the cannabis industry or those without the resources to hire professional assistance.

1. **Real Estate Challenges**: Finding and securing suitable real estate for cannabis operations can be difficult and expensive. Social equity applicants often face real estate prices that are well above market rates, partly due to the limited number of properties that meet the zoning and regulatory requirements for cannabis businesses.

2. **Bureaucratic Logjams**: Delays in the permitting process and other bureaucratic hurdles can stall the opening of a cannabis business. These delays can be costly and may result in the loss of property or other

opportunities.

3. **Lack of Resources**: Social equity applicants may lack the resources needed to navigate the cannabis industry successfully. This includes access to legal advice, business planning, and other professional services that are essential for establishing and running a cannabis business.

4. **Regulatory Challenges**: The cannabis industry is heavily regulated, and staying compliant with all the laws and regulations can be a significant challenge, especially for new entrants who may not be familiar with the intricacies of cannabis legislation.

5. **Market Saturation**: In some areas, the market may be saturated with cannabis businesses, making it difficult for new entrants, including social equity applicants, to gain a foothold and become profitable.

1. **Lack of Training**: Social equity applicants may not have access to the same level of training and education as other entrepreneurs in the cannabis industry, which can put them at a disadvantage.

Addressing these challenges is crucial for the success of social equity programs and for ensuring that the benefits of cannabis legalization are shared equitably. This may involve providing targeted support and resources to social equity applicants, simplifying the application process, and ensuring that these programs are adequately funded and managed.

PRO TIP: Access to capital is one of the biggest obstacles, be very diligent in seeking it!

Addressing the challenges faced by social equity programs in the cannabis industry requires a multifaceted approach. Here are some potential solutions:

1. **Increase Access to Capital**: Governments and private entities can provide grants, low-interest loans, and other financial assistance to social equity applicants. Partnerships with private investors interested in supporting social equity initiatives can also be encouraged.

2. **Simplify Application Processes**: Streamlining the licensing application process and providing clear guidelines can make it easier for social equity applicants to navigate the system. This could involve reducing paperwork and providing step-by-step guides.

3. **Provide Real Estate Assistance**: Governments could assist in securing suitable real estate for cannabis operations. This could involve creating a database of eligible properties or providing financial assistance for property acquisition.

4. **Reduce Bureaucratic Delays**: Governments

could streamline the permitting process and reduce bureaucratic hurdles. This could involve hiring more staff to process applications or creating a fast-track process for social equity applicants.

5. **Increase Support and Resources**: Providing ongoing support and resources to social equity applicants can help them navigate the cannabis industry successfully. This could involve offering free or low-cost legal advice, business planning services, and other professional services.

6. **Simplify Regulatory Compliance**: Governments could provide resources to help social equity applicants understand and comply with cannabis regulations. This could involve creating easy-to-understand guides or offering free compliance training.

7. **Control Market Saturation**: Governments could control the number of licenses issued to prevent market saturation. This could involve setting limits on the number of licenses issued in a certain area or prioritizing licenses for social equity applicants.

8. **Prevent Exploitation**: Governments could implement regulations to prevent the exploitation of social equity applicants by larger businesses. This could involve requiring a certain level of ownership and control by social equity applicants or conducting regular audits to ensure compliance.

These potential solutions aim to address the specific challenges faced by social equity programs in the cannabis industry. However, it's important to note that the effectiveness of these solutions can vary depending on the specific context and implementation. In conclusion, while social equity programs in the cannabis industry aim to promote diversity and address historical injustices, they face several criticisms and challenges. Addressing these issues is crucial to ensure the effectiveness of these programs and to achieve their intended goals.

As I read many books on guidelines and hearsay information, I found that people need to know specific stories about whats going on in these states. I did a little research and I wanted to share some real-world issues in trying to implement social equity programs, and some of the major markets. Let's take New York, for instance, the implementation of social equity cannabis licenses has faced several challenges, including legal disputes and operational issues.

One of the main issues has been the legal challenges against the state's Office of Cannabis Management (OCM) and the Cannabis Control Board. Several lawsuits have been filed, alleging discrimination and violation of the Constitution's Equal Protection Clause. For instance, a lawsuit filed by Valencia Ag LLC claimed that the social equity approach, which offers discounted licensing fees and other benefits to minority and women applicants, discriminates against white men. Another lawsuit argued that the state's Marijuana Regulation and Taxation Act, which legalized adult-use recreational cannabis in New York, was supposed to open applications to everyone at the same time, not just to a certain category of people. Another challenge has been the slow rollout of the program. As of August 2023, only 21 out of 463 approved social equity retail licenses were operational. This slow progress has been attributed to legal challenges over the state's permitting process, which have left more than 400 provisional licensees in limbo. The state has also been criticized for its handling of the Conditional Adult-Use Retail Dispensary (CAURD) licenses. A lawsuit alleged that state officials have been favoring "Justice Involved" individuals over disabled veterans in the licensing process. Despite these challenges, New York State has been making efforts to address these issues and improve the implementation of its social equity cannabis licenses. For instance, the state has broadened its licensing program to open it up to a more diverse pool of applicants. The state has also opened up a general application window to grow, process, distribute, or sell marijuana, which could potentially allow more businesses to enter the market. However, these efforts have also raised concerns. For example, the opening of the general application window has raised fears among farmers and retailers that they could be squeezed out by deeper-pocketed companies. [3]

Here are some of the more specific issues that social equity cannabis licenses in New York State have encountered:

1. **Legal Challenges**: There have been lawsuits filed against New York's Office of Cannabis Management (OCM) and the Cannabis Control Board, alleging discrimination and violation of the Constitution's Equal Protection Clause. For example, a lawsuit by Valencia Ag LLC claimed that the social equity approach discriminates against white men by providing business advantages for minority and women entrepreneurs.

2. **Slow Rollout**: The rollout of the social equity program has been slow, with only a fraction of the approved social equity retail licenses operational as of August 2023. Legal

challenges over the state's permitting process have contributed to this delay, leaving many provisional licensees in limbo.

3. **Residency Requirements**: A lawsuit challenged the residency requirements for social equity applicants, alleging that they favor New York residents and violate the federal Dormant Commerce Clause, which prevents states from discriminating against interstate commerce.

4. **Implementation Issues**: The state has been criticized for its handling of the Conditional Adult-Use Retail Dispensary (CAURD) licenses, with a lawsuit alleging that state officials have been favoring "Justice Involved" individuals over disabled veterans in the licensing process.

5. **Ratio of Licenses**: There is confusion among applicants regarding how the state will satisfy the ratio outlined in the Marijuana Regulation & Taxation Act, which specifies that 50% of permits should go to Social & Economic Equity (SEE) applicants. The concern is that the randomized selection process may not reflect the larger group of applicants.

6. **Market Entry for Large Corporations**: There is concern that the opening of the general application window for cannabis licenses could allow larger corporations to enter the market, potentially squeezing out smaller businesses, including those owned by social equity applicants.

7. **Prioritization of Social Equity Applicants**: The OCM's policy decision to prioritize social equity applicants has been a point of contention, with some arguing that it has contributed to the slow rollout of the legal cannabis market in New York.

These issues highlight the complexities and challenges of implementing a social equity program in the cannabis industry, particularly in a state with a large and diverse population like New York. The state has made efforts to address these challenges, such as broadening the licensing program to include a more diverse pool of applicants, but concerns remain about the effectiveness and fairness of the social equity program. [4]

I want readers to know that these issues are not just central to New York, many of the same issues have happened in other states as well. The social equity cannabis licensing program in Illinois has faced a series of challenges and controversies since its inception. The program was designed to prioritize social equity so that those most affected by decades of harsh drug policy had their chance to participate in the industry, not just massive corporations run by the already wealthy. Despite these intentions, the rollout has been fraught with issues. One of the main problems has been the slow pace of license issuance. As of November 2022, the Illinois Department of Financial and

Professional Regulation (IDFPR) had issued 192 conditional adult-use cannabis dispensing organization licenses from lotteries in 2021 and 2022, but only a fraction of these had become operational. This slow progress has been attributed to state delays, COVID delays, lawsuits, and red tape.

Legal challenges have also been a significant hurdle. Lawsuits have delayed the state's highly competitive social equity process, which was supposed to be a turning point for the industry. After these delays, Illinois finished awarding 185 licenses for cannabis dispensaries in mid-August 2022. However, the implementation of these licenses has been slow, and there have been calls for action from the state to address the delays and ensure that the social equity program fulfills its promises. Another issue has been the difficulty social equity applicants face in accessing capital and navigating the complex regulatory environment. Overcoming structural inequities through partnerships with financial institutions has been challenging, and the state's Department of Commerce and Economic Opportunity (DCEO) has been working to engage social equity licensees and work through these challenges.

Despite these challenges, the Pritzker Administration has made efforts to address them, such as announcing the results of a social equity criteria lottery to award additional conditional adult-use cannabis dispensing organization licenses[4]. The state has also made a significant commitment to community reinvestment, expunging criminal histories related to cannabis, and providing low-interest loans to qualified licensed companies through its Social Equity Cannabis Loan Program. However, the slow rollout of licenses and the operational challenges faced by social equity licensees have led to criticism and demands for more effective implementation of the program. The Alliance For Cannabis Equity, consisting of 17 organizations, has called on Illinois leaders to take action to support social equity entrepreneurs who have not yet been able to start their businesses despite the state seeing billions of dollars in sales.

I have attached some of the more specific challenges that Illinois applicants have faced, they have been significantly affected by the licensing process in several ways:

1. **Delays in License Issuance**: The process of issuing licenses to social equity applicants has been slow and fraught with delays. As of November 2022, the Illinois Department of Financial and Professional Regulation had issued 192 conditional adult-use cannabis dispensing organization licenses from lotteries in 2021 and 2022, but only a fraction of these had become operational.

2. **Legal Challenges**: The licensing process has been subject to numerous legal challenges, which have further delayed the issuance of licenses. These lawsuits have challenged various aspects of the licensing process, including the additional points awarded to Illinois residents as part of the application process.

3. **Access to Capital**: Social equity applicants have faced significant challenges in accessing the capital necessary to start and maintain their businesses. This has been a major barrier to the successful implementation of the social equity program.

4. **Regulatory Complexity**: Navigating the complex regulatory environment has been another significant challenge for social equity applicants. This includes understanding and complying with the specific requirements to qualify as a social equity applicant, such as having lived in a "disproportionately impacted area" for five of the last 10 years, with at least 50% of their employees also living in a disproportionately impacted area, or having been impacted by a cannabis-related offense.

5. **Operational Challenges**: Even after obtaining a license, social equity applicants have faced operational challenges that have delayed the opening of their businesses. These challenges include securing approved real estate, finding in-

vestors with the capital to build dispensaries, and navigating the state's regulatory process.

Despite these challenges, the state has made efforts to support social equity applicants, such as providing low-interest loans through its Social Equity Cannabis Loan Program and offering free licensing and post-licensing technical assistance. However, these efforts have not fully addressed the challenges faced by social equity applicants, and there have been calls for more effective implementation of the program. [5]

In summary, while Illinois has made history with its social equity cannabis program, the implementation has been marred by delays, legal challenges, and difficulties in accessing capital and navigating regulations. Efforts are ongoing to improve the program and support social equity applicants, but there is still a long way to go to achieve the intended goals of the program. [6]

Chapter 7

Social Equity Partnerships: Lightening the Load

P artnerships are a good way to get a leg up in the industry by teaming up with experienced people within the industry. I have partnered with a social equity group out of Illinois and they tell me all the time how grateful they are for the collaboration. We have seen so many social equity licensees lose their licenses from a lack of experience and knowledge. Social equity programs in the cannabis industry can form various partnerships to address the challenges they face. Here are some potential partnerships:

1. **Partnerships with Local Businesses and Farmers**: Social equity applicants can partner with local businesses and farmers to reinforce community connections and ensure that the benefits of the cannabis industry are shared locally. This can also help to counter the influence of large, profit-driven corporations and provide more sustainable, long-term benefits for social equity applicants and their communities.

2. **Joint Ventures**: Some social equity programs, like the Marijuana Regulatory Agency's Joint Ventures Program, have created partnerships between social equity applicants

and existing cannabis businesses. These partnerships can provide social equity applicants with the necessary funding and technical assistance to establish and run a cannabis business.

1. **Employment Partnerships**: Cannabis companies can form strategic partnerships with organizations inside and outside the industry to create job
   opportunities for people from marginalized communities. This can help to diversify the workforce and
   bring more people into the cannabis sector.

2. **Partnerships with Cannabis Tech Providers**:
   Cannabis tech providers like Flowhub offer Social
   Equity Programs that provide support to underrepresented dispensary owners, including minority-owned, woman-owned, or veteran-owned businesses. These partnerships can help to remove hurdles
   to entry for these entrepreneurs.

3. **Partnerships with Public Relations Firms**: Public relations firms like NisonCo, which grew from advocacy, uphold ideals of social justice in their work and can partner with social equity programs to further their mission and reach.

These partnerships can provide social equity applicants with the resources, support, and opportunities they need to successfully enter the cannabis industry. However, it's important to ensure that these partnerships are genuine and beneficial for all parties involved and that they truly support the goals of social equity. [7]

PRO TIP: A good partnership can be invaluable, having someone there to share the burden can be the difference between success and failure

1. **Detroit Cannabis Project**: In Detroit, the Detroit Cannabis Project was created to provide technical and financial knowledge to social equity applicants. The project, which is a partnership between the city and local businesses, has trained close to 300 social equity applicants through weekly webinars on operations, marketing, and compliance.

2. **Local Partnerships in New York**: Social equity applicants have partnered with local businesses and hemp farmers in New York. These partnerships reinforce community connections and ensure that the benefits of the cannabis industry are shared locally. Local enterprises have a deeper understanding of their communities, fostering trust and goodwill.

3. **Marijuana Regulatory Agency Joint Ventures Program**: The Marijuana Regulatory Agency's Joint Ventures Program has created partnerships between social equity applicants and existing cannabis businesses. These partnerships provide social equity applicants with the necessary funding and technical assistance to successfully establish and run a cannabis business.

4. **Flowhub Social Equity Program**: Flowhub, a cannabis tech provider, offers a Social Equity Program that provides support to underrepresented dispensary owners, including minority-owned, woman-owned, or veteran-owned businesses. This program aims to remove hurdles to entry for these entrepreneurs.

5. **Confia Social Equity Program**: Confia, a financial services provider, has partnered with key organizations to provide compliant and affordable financial services to small businesses and leaders who have endured inequality in the cannabis industry.

6. **Issue 2 in Ohio**: Issue 2 in Ohio includes a social equity and jobs program that favors economically or socially disadvantaged individuals. This program has been welcomed by many local cannabis entrepreneurs who believe it will help small businesses grow.

These partnerships have helped to foster business opportunities for women and people of color, provided job training and business support, and have begun to bridge the access gap for previously marginalized communities. However, it's important to note that while these partnerships have had successes, they also face challenges such as limited access to capital, complex application processes, and the need for ongoing support and resources for social equity applicants. [8]

Partnerships can really take the fear of jumping into a new and unfamiliar industry away. I want this book to be more in layman's terms for my readers. So I put together two sets of Fictional and Non-fictional scenarios to give you some real-world examples as well as some possible partnership structures so that you can get an idea of how this can help you.

Fictional Story

The Scenario

Imagine a social equity applicant, John, who has been awarded a license to operate a cannabis dispensary in Illinois. He decides to form a partnership with a multi-state cannabis operator, Canopy Growth Corporation.

The Partnership Structure

- **John's Dispensary**: Holds the social equity license and provides the retail space. John brings his knowledge of the local community and his passion for cannabis education and social justice.

- **Canopy Growth Corporation**: Brings its extensive

experience in the cannabis industry, including operations, marketing, and regulatory compliance.

How Each Member Helps the Other

- **John's Dispensary**:

  - Provides Canopy Growth with a foothold in the Illinois market, which is part of its expansion strategy.

  - Offers insights into the needs of social equity customers, helping Canopy Growth tailor its products and marketing strategies.

- **Canopy Growth Corporation**:

  - Provides John with operational expertise, marketing support, and regulatory guidance.

  - Assists with capital investment, helping John to set up his dispensary and manage operational costs.

The Outcome

The partnership allows John to successfully launch and operate his dispensary, attracting more customers and generating higher revenue. Canopy Growth benefits from the expansion into a new market and the opportunity to demonstrate its commitment to social equity in the cannabis industry.

Non-Fictional Story

The Scenario

In Massachusetts, a social equity applicant, Leah Daniels, partnered with a multi-state operator, Sira Naturals, to open a cannabis dispensary.

The Partnership Structure

- **Leah Daniels**: Holds the social equity license and provides the retail space. Leah brings her knowledge of the local community and her passion for cannabis education and social justice.

- **Sira Naturals**: Brings its extensive experience in the cannabis industry, including operations, marketing, and regulatory compliance.

How Each Member Helps the Other

- **Leah Daniels**:

  - Provides Sira Naturals with a foothold in the Massachusetts market, which is part of their expansion strategy.

  - Offers insights into the needs of social equity customers, helping Sira Naturals tailor its products and marketing strategies.

- **Sira Naturals**:

  - Provides Leah with operational expertise, marketing support, and regulatory guidance.

  - Assists with capital investment, helping Leah to

set up her dispensary and manage operational costs.

The Outcome

The partnership allowed Leah to successfully launch and operate her dispensary, attracting more customers and generating higher revenue. Sira Naturals benefited from the expansion into a new market and the opportunity to demonstrate its commitment to social equity in the cannabis industry.

Fictional Story:

Meet Maya, a social equity cannabis licensee who has been granted a cannabis license in her state. Maya is passionate about building a successful cannabis business but lacks the necessary capital and expertise to get started. On the other hand, Greenleaf Enterprises, a well-established and highly capitalized multi-state cannabis operator, sees the potential in partnering with social equity licensees to promote diversity and inclusivity within the industry. Maya and Greenleaf Enterprises come together and decide to form a partnership. They establish a clear framework for their business collaboration, with a focus on mutual benefits and shared values.

Here's how they structure their partnership:

1. Capital Injection: Greenleaf Enterprises agrees to provide the necessary capital to fund Maya's business operations. This includes financing her cultivation facility setup, securing inventory, and covering other startup costs. In return, Greenleaf will have an ownership stake in the business, but the terms ensure that Maya retains control and decision-making authority.

2. Operational Support: Greenleaf brings valuable operational expertise to the partnership. They assist Maya in developing efficient cultivation and manufacturing processes, implementing quality control measures, and adhering to regulatory compliance. Greenleaf's experience and industry knowledge become instrumental in ensuring Maya's business operates smoothly and efficiently.

3. Branding and Marketing: Maya recognizes Greenleaf's established brand and marketing capabilities. Greenleaf helps Maya in creating a compelling brand identity and marketing strategy, which aligns with the values of the social equity li-

cense program. Together, they develop marketing campaigns that highlight their commitment to diversity, community engagement, and high-quality cannabis products.

4. Compliance and Regulatory Guidance: Greenleaf has an experienced compliance team well-versed in navigating complex regulations in multiple states. They lend their expertise to ensure that Maya's business adheres to all the relevant local and state regulations. This guidance minimizes the risk of compliance issues and ensures a smooth operation within the legal framework.

5. Job Creation and Community Involvement: The partnership places a strong emphasis on creating job opportunities for individuals from marginalized communities. Maya and Greenleaf collaborate on job training programs to ensure that underrepresented individuals have the necessary skills to thrive in the industry. Additionally, they work together to offer community outreach initiatives, such as supporting local nonprofits and social equity initiatives.

Non-fictional Story:

In a real-world example, PharmaGrow, a social equity cannabis license holder, partnered with Terraco Holdings, a well-established multi-state cannabis operator. Together, they formed a successful cannabis business partnership in Massachusetts.

Here's how they structured their partnership:

1. Capital and Operational Support: Terraco Holdings provided the necessary funding for PharmaGrow's cultivation facility setup and expansion. They also offered operational support, leveraged their industry experience, and assisted in implementing efficient cultivation practices.

2. Branding and Marketing: Terraco Holdings had an established brand and marketing strategy, which they extended to PharmaGrow. They collaborated on branding initiatives, packaging design, and marketing campaigns to position PharmaGrow as a unique and socially responsible player in the Massachusetts cannabis market.

3. Compliance and Regulatory Assistance: PharmaGrow received guidance from Terraco's compliance team to ensure their operations complied with state and local regulations. Terraco helped PharmaGrow navigate the complex licensing and regulatory landscape in Massachusetts.

4. Community Engagement: As part of their partnership, PharmaGrow and Terraco prioritized creating job opportunities for individuals from communities disproportionately impacted by the war on drugs. They implemented training programs and actively recruited individuals who qualified under social equity criteria, contributing to the economic empowerment of marginalized communities.

By partnering with an established multi-state operator like Terraco Holdings, PharmaGrow was able to overcome common challenges faced by social equity license holders. The partnership allowed them to leverage industry expertise, access capital, establish a strong brand presence, and contribute positively to their local community. It's important to note that the specific terms and structures of partnerships can vary widely based on the needs and goals of the parties involved.

Proper legal and business advice should always be sought when entering into any business partnership agreement.

PRO TIP: Every licensee will have its strengths and its weaknesses, Choose a partner that completes you- Just like in a real relationship!

Chapter 8

Social Equity Licenses: A Head Start to Cashing In on the Cannabis Industry

Hopefully, in the previous chapters, you all have learned how to participate in the social equity process. I want to finish with this chapter on how to utilize this social equity license, and or partnership to make millions in this business before the multi-state operators are allowed to come in and overtake the cannabis small business industry.

One of the biggest advantages of a social equity license in most of the newer states that have allowed recreational or medical cannabis to be allowed in their state is that they give social equity licenses a time to operate before they allow the multi-state operators, who are heavily capitalized to enter the market. This is a big opportunity for the social equity licenses to establish themselves, their products, and their brands in the market. Usually, the consumer, based on my almost 20 years as a Dispensary owner in California, likes to shop at the same place. Because cannabis is still a Schedule I drug and is sometimes frowned upon by certain people and or groups, customers like to be private about their purchases. This means if they are comfortable going to one location and choosing a brand, they like to stick with it. This is a big deal and a great opportunity for social equity licenses that have been allowed to operate, before the big boys come in, can establish a relationship and their brand amongst the citizens of that particular state so that when the big guys come in they won't automatically dominate the customer base.

PRO TIP: Being first to market gives you a big leg up on the competition. Don't wait to release multiple brands – Get in the game!

Another big advantage of having a social equity license is that because multistate operators cannot come into the market, until after the social equity licenses have had a chance to open up, usually a one or two-year span, that gives a social equity licensee a big opportunity to negotiate partnerships with some of these major operators. Because the major operators know the importance of branding and getting a product into a market first they will typically team up and partner with a social equity license, and this helps with the capitalization problems that most social equity applicants have because of the lack of banking.

Here are some key advantages:

1. Access to Capital: One significant advantage is the access to capital that a highly capitalized MSO can provide. Social equity cannabis licensees often face financial limitations, but partnering with a well-funded MSO can provide the necessary funding for expansion, operations, and infrastructure development.

2. Operational Expertise: MSOs typically have extensive experience and expertise in all aspects of running a cannabis business, including cultivation, manufacturing, distribution, and retail operations. By partnering with an MSO, social equity licensees can benefit from their proven operational strategies and industry knowledge.

3. Compliance and Regulatory Support: Compliance with the complex and ever-evolving regulations in the cannabis industry is crucial. MSOs often have dedicated compliance teams that can assist with navigating the regulatory landscape, ensuring that operations align with local and state laws. This support can be invaluable to social equity licensees, who may have limited experience dealing with compliance matters.

4. Branding and Marketing Support: MSOs often have established brands and marketing strategies, which can help social equity licensees gain brand recognition and market share. Leveraging the MSO's marketing expertise, social equity licensees can benefit from increased visibility, customer acquisition, and brand development.

PRO TIP: Getting a brand established even if you have to do a CBD brand is crucial to getting ahead of the competition.

1. Network and Distribution Channels: MSOs often have an extensive network of distribution channels, including established relationships with suppliers, dispensaries, and vendors. Through a partnership, social equity licensees can leverage these networks to enhance their distribution capabilities, expand market reach, and gain access to a larger customer base.

2. Job Creation and Diversity: Partnering with an MSO can help social equity licensees create more job opportunities. MSOs often have larger teams and can provide training and employment opportunities to individuals designated by social equity initiatives,

thereby promoting diversity and equality within the cannabis industry.

PRO TIP: Teaming up with the right MSO can set you apart from the competition. MSOs seek relationships with SE licenses because most states give out SE licenses first with a 1 to 2-year window before regular licenses are open to the public.

It's important to note that finding the right partner is crucial, as the partnership should align with the social equity licensee's values, objectives, and goals. Proper due diligence and legal assistance should be sought when entering into any partnership agreement.

So, hopefully, the plethora of information that I have given you on the social equity process, challenges, and solutions, will help you in your endeavor into the social equity aspect of the cannabis industry. If you are a social equity licensee holder, definitely take advantage of some of those inside tips, so that you can be successful in this billion-dollar industry and make the most of it! [9]

I want to leave you with a fictional but realistic potential outcome of a situation if you follow the advice that I've given you so far!

Meet Sarah, a passionate entrepreneur and recipient of a social equity cannabis license in a state that recently legalized recreational marijuana. Sarah grew up in a marginalized community impacted by the war on drugs and was determined to build a successful cannabis business while also giving back to her community.

In the beginning, Sarah faced numerous obstacles. Firstly, she struggled to secure sufficient funding to launch her business. Traditional lenders were hesitant to provide loans to cannabis startups due to ongoing regulatory challenges and the stigma surrounding the industry. However, through perseverance and applying for specialized grants and social equity programs, Sarah managed to secure enough capital to commence her operations.

Next, Sarah faced the daunting task of navigating the complex web of state and local regulations. The licensing process proved to be lengthy and bureaucratic, with countless paperwork and compliance requirements. Fortunately, Sarah sought legal advice and partnered with a knowledgeable industry consultant who guided her through the process, ensuring that she met all the necessary requirements while avoiding costly pitfalls.

Once Sarah obtained her license, she encountered difficulties setting up her cultivation facility. Locating an appropriate property with the necessary infrastructure at an affordable price proved challenging. However, she started networking with other industry professionals and found a local real estate partner who was willing to provide her with a suitable space and help with facility development.

However, Sarah's obstacles didn't end there. She faced challenges in sourcing quality genetics, securing reliable suppliers, and developing efficient cultivation practices. These obstacles were exacerbated by limited industry connections and a lack of experience in the cannabis sector. In response, Sarah actively sought out mentorship programs, attended industry events, and joined networking groups to connect with experienced growers and operators. Despite the hurdles, Sarah's perseverance and dedication paid off. She successfully cultivated her first crop and established strategic partnerships with other local cannabis businesses, allowing her to distribute her products to dispensaries. Sarah developed a strong brand identity centered around quality, community engagement, and social responsibility.

Over time, Sarah's business thrived, and she became a respected figure in the industry and her community. She established job training programs that targeted individuals from marginalized communities, helping to combat the historical disparities caused by the war on drugs. Her business not only created employment opportunities but also contributed a portion of its profits to local community development projects, educational scholarships, and drug rehabilitation programs. Sarah's success story became an inspiration for other social equity licensees and budding entrepreneurs who shared her vision for a well-regulated, inclusive cannabis industry. As the cannabis market continued to grow and evolve, Sarah's business expanded into multiple states, offering even more job opportunities and giving back to new communities.

Sarah's journey demonstrates the challenges faced by social equity cannabis licensees but also highlights the potential for success when coupled with determination, mentoring, partnership, and a commitment to social responsibility.

BE LIKE SARAH!

1. https://www.forbes.com/sites/roberthoban/2020/08/31/t

   he-critical-importance-of-social-equi-
   ty-in-the-cannabis-in dustry/
   https://portal.ct.gov/cannabis/knowledge-base/categori
   e s/social-equity/social-equity-definitions
   https://cannabis.ny.gov/system/files/documents/2022/
   0
   2/cannabis-management-fact-sheet-social-equi-
   ty_0_0.pdf
   https://cannabis.ca.gov/resources/equity/
   https://flowhub.com/cannabis-social-equity-programs-
   complete-guide
   https://www.nj.gov/cannabis/resources/faqs/social-eq-
   uity/
   https://www.michigan.gov/cra/sections/social-equi-
   ty-program
   https://www.healthline.com/health/social-equi-
   ty-in-cannabis

2. https://www.brookings.edu/articles/state-cannabis-re-
for

m-is-putting-social-justice-front-and-center/

https://pubmed.ncbi.nlm.nih.gov/31634005/

https://www.forbes.com/sites/roberthoban/2020/08/31/t

he-critical-importance-of-social-equi-
ty-in-the-cannabis-industry/

https://learnaboutsam.org/social-justice/

https://thecannabisindustry.org/social-justice-and-equi
ty-in-the-cannabis-industry-2/

https://www.americanbar.org/groups/crsj/publica-
tions/h

uman_rights_magazine_home/economic-is-
sues-in-criminal

-justice/social-equity-in-marijuana-regulation/

https://www.ncbi.nlm.nih.gov/pmc/articles/PMC1037
310 4/

https://www.aclu.org/news/criminal-law-reform/mari-
ju

ana-legalization-racial-justice-issue

4. Citations:

5. Citations:

6. Citations:

7. https://flowhub.com/cannabis-social-equity-programs-complete-guide
https://www.nydailynews.com/2023/11/08/social-equi-ty-
in-cannabis-needs-local-partners/
https://mjbizdaily.com/cannabis-companies-can-create-social-impact-through-employment-partnerships/
https://vangst.com/blog/vangst-partners-with-cannabis

-business-office
https://www.ctinsider.com/cannabis/article/critics-say-cannabis-equity-partnerships-favor-18272300.php
https://nisonco.com/cannabis-industry-social-equity-st
rategies/

8. https://mjbizdaily.com/small-scale-cannabis-social-equity-success-stories/
   https://www.nydailynews.com/2023/11/08/social-equity-in-cannabis-needs-local-partners/
   https://flowhub.com/cannabis-social-equity-programs-complete-guide
   https://www.confia.io/social-equity-program/

   https://signalcleveland.org/how-issue-2-proposes-to-help-small-businesses-in-the-marijuana-industry/
   https://cannabis.ca.gov/resources/equity/
   https://www.ctinsider.com/cannabis/article/critics-say-cannabis-equity-partnerships-favor-18272300.php

9. https://mjbizdaily.com/small-scale-cannabis-social-equity-success-stories/

   https://www.nydailynews.com/2023/11/08/social-equity-in-cannabis-needs-local-partners/

   https://flowhub.com/cannabis-social-equity-programs-complete-guide

   https://www.confia.io/social-equity-program/

   https://signalcleveland.org/how-issue-2-proposes-to-help-small-businesses-in-the-marijuana-industry/

   https://cannabis.ca.gov/resources/equity/

   https://www.ctinsider.com/cannabis/article/critics-say-cannabis-equity-partnerships-favor-18272300.php

Acknowledgements

First, I would like to acknowledge my family, Toni, Jahkeem, and Leedia, for always giving me the inspiration to keep moving forward. I'd also like to thank my parents Josephine and Willie and all my brothers and sisters, who keep me sharp and focused on becoming successful.

Next, I would like to thank the cannabis industry for allowing me to participate and for being fearful in the eyes of controversy. I would like to thank the ever-evolving technology that helps regular guys like myself utilize technology so that we can put our words into books.

Last, but not least, I would like to thank the God within, and the ever-present God within the universe, the creator, for keeping me motivated to do the actual work!

www.ingramcontent.com/pod-product-compliance
Lightning Source LLC
Chambersburg PA
CBHW060254030426
42335CB00014B/1695